Chipmunk's Hole

by Dee Phillips

Consultants:

Suzy Gazlay, MA
Recipient, Presidential Award for Excellence in Science Teaching

Leah Birmingham, RVT
Assistant Director, Sandy Pines Wildlife Centre, Napanee, Ontario, Canada

Kimberly Brenneman, PhD
National Institute for Early Education Research, Rutgers University, New Brunswick, New Jersey

BEARPORT
PUBLISHING

New York, New York

Credits

Cover, © Renaud Thomas/Shutterstock and © Margaret M. Stewart/Shutterstock; 3, © kompasstudio/ Shutterstock; 4L, © Chas/Shutterstock; 4R, © Renaud Thomas/Shutterstock; 5, © Renaud Thomas/Shutterstock; 6R, © Corbis/Shutterstock; 6L, © Cosmographics; 7, © Steve Byland/Shutterstock; 8, © Eric Isselée/Shutterstock; 9, © Ruby Tuesday Books Ltd; 10TL, © Carolyn Brule/ Shutterstock; 10TR, © Kert/Shutterstock; 10BL, © Denis Pepin/Shutterstock; 10BR, © Mark Bridger/Shutterstock; 11, © Ryan M. Bolton/ Shutterstock; 12, © Margaret M. Stewart/Shutterstock; 13TL, © Chris Pole/Shutterstock; 13TC, © Denis Dore/Shutterstock; 13TC, © Pakhnyushcha/Shutterstock; 13TR, © Charles F. McCarthy/Shutterstock; 13BL, © Givaga/Shutterstock; 13BC, © Samokhin/Shutterstock; 14, © Gary Carter/Corbis; 15, © S. & D. & K. Maslowski/FLPA; 17, © Breck P. Kent/Animals Animals; 18–19, © Don Chernoff/www. dcwild.com; 20, © Margaret M. Stewart/Shutterstock; 21, © Margaret M. Stewart/Shutterstock; 22BL, © Eric Isselée/Shutterstock; 22BR, © Ruby Tuesday Books Ltd; 23TL, © Renaud Thomas/Shutterstock; 23TR, © Margaret M. Stewart/Shutterstock; 23BL, © Kert/ Shutterstock; 23BR, © Sally Wallis/Shutterstock.

Publisher: Kenn Goin
Editorial Director: Adam Siegel
Creative Director: Spencer Brinker
Design: Alix Wood
Editor: Mark J. Sachner
Photo Researcher: Ruby Tuesday Books Ltd

Library of Congress Cataloging-in-Publication Data

Phillips, Dee, 1967–
  Chipmunk's hole / by Dee Phillips.
      p. cm. — (The hole truth! Underground animal life)
  Includes bibliographical references and index.
  ISBN-13: 978-1-61772-407-7 (library binding)
  ISBN-10: 1-61772-407-6 (library binding)
  1. Chipmunks—Habitations—Juvenile literature. I. Title.
  QL737.R68P45 2012
  599.36'4—dc23
                          2011044052

For more information, write to Bearport Publishing Company, Inc., 45 West 21st Street, Suite 3B, New York, New York 10010. Printed in the United States of America in North Mankato, Minnesota.

10 9 8 7 6 5 4 3 2 1

Contents

Welcome to a Chipmunk's Home

It is summer in the woods.

Suddenly, a chipmunk pops out of a hole between some rocks.

The hole is the entrance to the little animal's **burrow**.

burrow

Deep underground, the chipmunk has been digging a new home.

When its work is done, the chipmunk will sleep, eat, and stay safe in this secret hideaway.

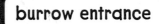

burrow entrance

chipmunk

The entrance hole
to a chipmunk's burrow
measures about two inches
(5 cm) across.

Check Out a Chipmunk!

Chipmunks are a type of **squirrel**.

Some kinds of chipmunks live in burrows.

Others make homes inside trees or logs.

Eastern chipmunks dig burrows in woods, parks, and backyards.

eastern chipmunk

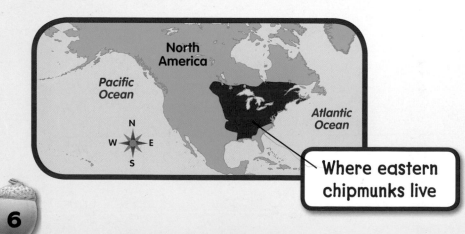

North America

Pacific Ocean

Atlantic Ocean

N
W · E
S

Where eastern chipmunks live

Sometimes eastern chipmunks dig burrows under people's garages or under tool sheds in backyards.

This adult eastern chipmunk is life-size. Use a ruler to measure the length of its body. Describe what the animal looks like.

Busy Builders

An adult chipmunk digs a cozy burrow where it lives by itself.

The little animal begins work by using its claws to dig an entrance hole.

Then it digs a long tunnel, some rooms, and extra holes for going in and out.

One of the rooms will be used as a bedroom.

Others will be used for storing food.

claws

Staying Safe Underground

Many animals hunt chipmunks for food.

A secret, underground home is a good place to hide from these **predators**.

A chipmunk must leave its burrow, however, to find food.

If an animal tries to catch it while it's outside, a chipmunk can scamper back down its hole.

A fox or pet cat will be too big to follow the chipmunk into its home!

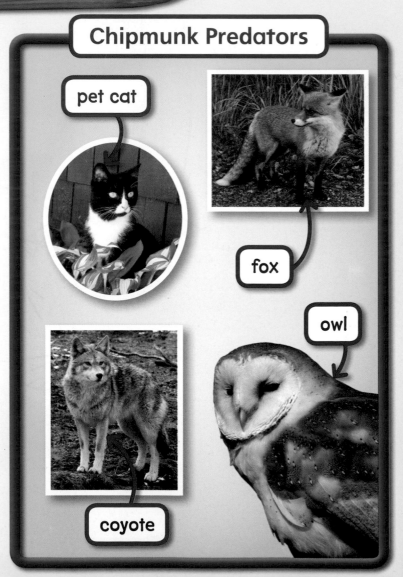

Chipmunk Predators

pet cat

fox

owl

coyote

Small predators, such as snakes, might get into a chipmunk's burrow through the entrance hole. If this happens, the chipmunk escapes out of one of the burrow's other holes.

Hungry Chipmunks

At night, chipmunks sleep in their underground bedrooms.

During the day, they look for food in the woods or backyards where they live.

Chipmunks mainly eat seeds, nuts, and berries.

They eat some of the food they find right away.

They also bring food back to their burrows and put it in their storerooms.

How do you think this chipmunk is carrying food?

Chipmunk Foods

berries

nuts

seeds from bird feeders

snail

mushrooms

Sometimes chipmunks eat mushrooms, birds' eggs, and small animals, such as insects, baby birds, and snails.

13

Chipmunk Cheeks

Chipmunks carry food in their cheeks.

They have a pouch, like a pocket, inside each cheek.

The busiest time of year for these little animals is fall.

Every day, each chipmunk carries hundreds of nuts and seeds back to its burrow.

By the end of fall, a chipmunk may have thousands of nuts and seeds stored underground!

Why do you think chipmunks store food in the fall?

A chipmunk can stuff 32 beechnuts into its cheek pouches at once!

life-size beechnut

a chipmunk in its storeroom

15

A Chipmunk's Winter

Chipmunks store food in the fall because there is not much food around in winter.

When winter comes, chipmunks go underground into their warm burrows and stay there until spring.

They spend the cold winter sleeping in cozy beds made from leaves.

When they get hungry, they wake up and eat some food from their storerooms.

What do you think will happen when spring comes and the weather gets warmer?

In winter, a chipmunk may sleep for up to two weeks without waking up to eat.

A Burrow for Babies!

Spring is the time when chipmunks leave their burrows to look for food again.

It is also the time when male and female chipmunks **mate**.

About four weeks after mating, a female chipmunk gives birth to her babies in her burrow.

She has four or five babies at one time.

The babies' eyes are closed and they cannot see.

The mother chipmunk feeds the babies milk from her body.

three-week-old chipmunk

An adult chipmunk weighs about three ounces (85 g). That's the same weight as 15 quarters. A newborn baby chipmunk weighs less than one quarter!

Meet a Chipmunk Family!

Chipmunk babies do not go outside the burrow until they are six weeks old.

By this time, the babies have fur and their eyes are open.

They look like an adult, but they are smaller.

The babies are ready to eat nuts, fruit, and other adult foods.

In about two weeks, each young chipmunk will go off and dig its own burrow!

a baby chipmunk eating a strawberry

A chipmunk baby begins to grow fur at ten days old. Its eyes open after about 30 days.

baby chipmunks

Science Lab

Be a Chipmunk Scientist!

Imagine you are a scientist who studies chipmunks.

Write a report to tell other people all about a chipmunk's home.

Use the information in this book to help you.

Draw pictures to include in your report.

When you are finished, present your report to your friends and family.

Here are some words that you can use when writing or talking about chipmunk homes.

burrow | tunnel | leaves

storeroom | entrance hole

predators | nuts | claws

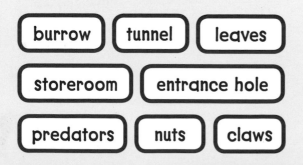

Read the questions below and think about the answers.

You can include some of the information from your answers in your report.

- *How does a chipmunk build its home?*

- *What rooms are in a chipmunk's home?*

- *Why is it a good idea for a chipmunk to live underground?*

- *How does a chipmunk get ready for winter?*

Science Words

burrow (BUR-oh)
a hole or tunnel dug by
an animal to live in

mate (MAYT) to come
together in order to have
young

predators (PRED-uh-turz)
animals that hunt and eat
other animals

squirrel (SKWUR-uhl)
a rodent with a bushy
tail that lives in burrows
or trees

Index

Read More

Fowler, Allan. *Squirrels and Chipmunks.* New York: Scholastic (2001).

Kalman, Bobbie. *Baby Chipmunks (It's Fun to Learn About Baby Animals).* New York: Crabtree (2011).

Sebastian, Emily. *Chipmunks (Animals Underground).* New York: PowerKids Press (2012).

Learn More Online

To learn more about chipmunks, visit **www.bearportpublishing.com/TheHoleTruth**

About the Author

Dee Phillips lives near the ocean on the southwest coast of England. She writes nonfiction and fiction books for children. Dee's biggest ambition is to one day walk the entire coast of Britain—it will take about ten months!